London   Museum of London   1985

Hugh Chapman
Jenny Hall
Geoffrey Marsh

THE LONDON WALL W

INTRODUCTION

The London Wall Walk follows the original line of the City Wall for much of its length, from the royal fortress of the Tower of London to the Museum of London, situated in the modern high-rise development of the Barbican. Between these two landmarks the Wall Walk passes surviving pieces of the Wall visible tó the public and the sites of the gates now buried deep beneath the City streets. It also passes close to eight of the surviving forty-one City churches.

The Walk is $1\frac{3}{4}$ miles (2.8km) long and is marked by twenty-one panels which can be followed in either direction. Completion of the Walk will take between one and two hours. Wheelchairs can reach most individual sites although access is difficult at some points.

AD 100

AD 200

AD 750

AD 1300

AD 1500

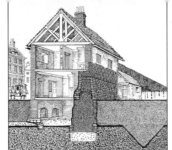

AD 1700

AD 1900

AD 1984

For nearly fifteen hundred years the physical growth of the City of London was limited by its defensive wall. The first Wall was built by the Romans c.AD 200, one hundred and fifty years after the foundation of *Londinium*. It stretched for 2 miles (3.2km), incorporating a pre-existing fort. In the 4th century the Romans strengthened the defences with towers on the eastern section of the Wall.

The Roman Wall formed the foundation of the later City Wall. During the Saxon period the Wall decayed but successive medieval and Tudor rebuildings and repairs restored it as a defensive wall. With the exception of a medieval realignment in the Blackfriars' area, the Wall retained its original line unaltered over the centuries. From the 17th century, as London expanded rapidly in size, the Wall was no longer necessary for defence. Much of it was demolished in the 18th and 19th centuries and where sections survived they became buried under shops and warehouses. During the 20th century several sections have been revealed by excavations and preserved.

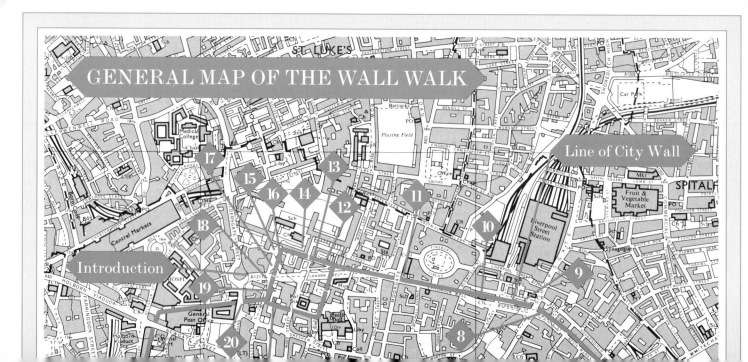

GENERAL MAP OF THE WALL WALK

Line of City Wall

Introduction

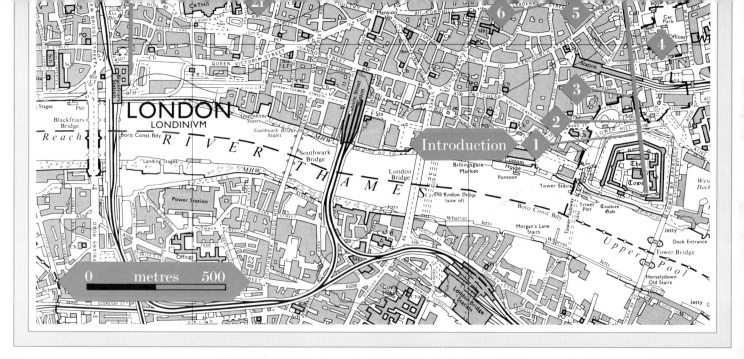

THE TOWER, *POSTERN GATE*

1

At south end of Tower Hill underpass

Excavations in 1979 revealed a medieval postern gate, positioned on the northern edge of the Tower of London moat. The moat was dug in the 1270s and the gate was probably built soon afterwards, perhaps replacing an earlier structure. It was smaller than the main City gates and was intended for pedestrian access.

The gate was well-built and the stone used for the detailed stonework came from Caen in Normandy. The settings and iron hinges for two gates survive with a portcullis slot in front. Arrowslits allowed covering fire from archers.

The proximity of the Tower moat, then filled with water, was disastrous since the gate's foundations were undermined. In 1440 the gate partially collapsed. A contemporary record noted '*the postern be-syde the Towre sanke downe into erthe vii fete.*'

The gate was resited and partly rebuilt to the north but '*such was their negligence . . . they suffered a weake and wooden building to be there made inhabited by persons of lewde life.*' The gate became derelict and finally disappeared in the 18th century.

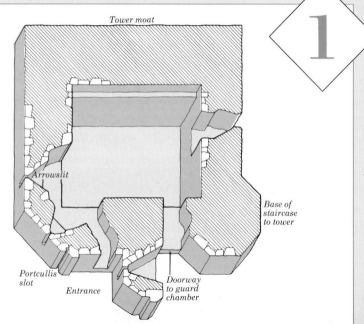

The Tower postern gate, as revealed by excavations.

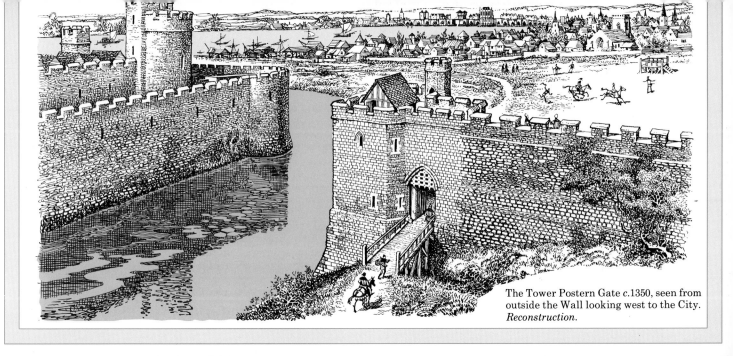

The Tower Postern Gate *c.*1350, seen from outside the Wall looking west to the City. *Reconstruction.*

TOWER HILL, *CITY WALL*

In garden to east of north entrance of Tower Hill underpass

This impressive section of wall still stands to a height of 35 feet (10.6m). The Roman work survives to the level of the sentry walk, 14½ feet (4.4m) high, with medieval stonework above. The Wall was constructed with coursed blocks of ragstone which sandwiched a rubble and mortar core. Layers of flat red tiles were used at intervals to give extra strength and stability. Complete with its battlements the Roman Wall would have been about 20 feet (6.3m) high. Outside the Wall was a defensive ditch.

To the north is the site of one of the towers added to the outside of the Wall in the 4th century. Stones recovered from its foundations in 1852 and 1935 included part of the memorial inscription from the tomb of Julius Classicianus, the Roman Provincial Procurator (financial administrator) in AD 61.

In the medieval period the defences were repaired and heightened. The stonework was more irregular with a sentry walk only 3 feet (0.9m) wide. To the west was the site of the Tower Hill scaffold where many famous prisoners were publicly beheaded, the last in 1747.

Dismantling the late Roman tower on the outside of the City Wall in 1852. 19th century engraving.

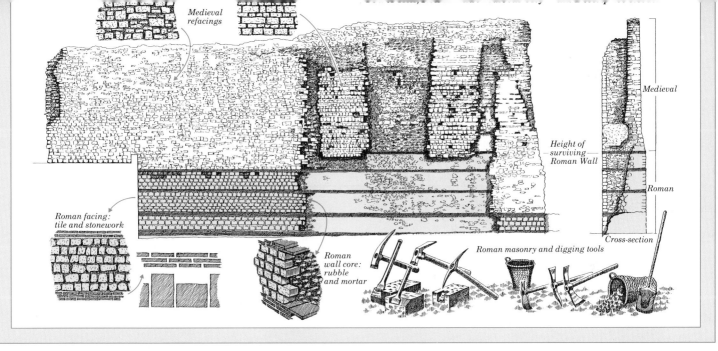

Medieval
refacings

Medieval

Height of
surviving
Roman Wall

Roman

Cross-section

Roman facing:
tile and stonework

Roman
wall core:
rubble
and mortar

Roman masonry and digging tools

COOPER'S ROW, *CITY WALL*

In courtyard by bank building

The Wall survives here to a height of 35 feet (10.6m). The lower section, 14½ feet (4.4m), is Roman and stands to the height of the sentry walk. The characteristic red tile and ragstone can be seen and at the base on the outer face the red sandstone plinth which marks Roman ground level. During the medieval period the Wall was heightened by 21 feet (6.2m) with irregular masonry which narrowed to a sentry walk 3 feet (0.9m) wide. At the same time the ditch outside the Wall was redug and broadened.

A double staircase led to the medieval sentry walk. On either side are loopholes which could be used by archers. There is no surviving means of access and the loopholes were probably reached by a timber platform keyed into the socket holes which are visible. There is no parallel for this arrangement elsewhere on the Wall, indicating the special care taken with defences close to the Tower. The outer face gives a good impression of the original strength of London's defences.

Medieval archer firing through a loophole in the Wall

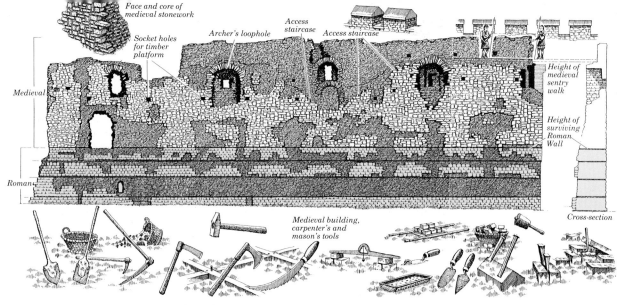

Face and core of
medieval stonework

Socket holes
for timber
platform

Archer's loophole

Access
staircase

Access
staircase

Height of
medieval
sentry
walk

Medieval

Height of
surviving
Roman
Wall

Roman

Cross-section

Medieval building,
carpenter's and
mason's tools

Cooper's Row, Roman and Medieval City Wall. *Descriptive elevation.*

EMPEROR HOUSE, *CITY WALL*

Outside entrance and at rear of building

Excavations in 1979–80 revealed a 32 feet (10m) length of the Roman City Wall. The red sandstone plinth at the base marks the position of Roman ground level. Above are layers of ragstone with bonding courses of red tiles. Outside the Wall was a V-shaped defensive ditch 16 feet (4.8m) wide. The earth from this was used to form a supporting bank on the inner side of the Wall.

In the troubled years of the later 4th century at least twenty towers were added to the eastern side of the City Wall. These towers, probably 26 to 30 feet (8–9m) high, provided a platform for catapults. The ditch was also filled in and a larger one dug further away from the Wall.

The base of one of these Roman towers can be seen. The towers were built from ragstone, crushed chalk and tombstones removed from nearby cemeteries. The builders stepped the foundations into the earlier ditch to prevent subsidence. Many of the towers were re-used in the medieval defences but this one had been demolished by the 13th century.

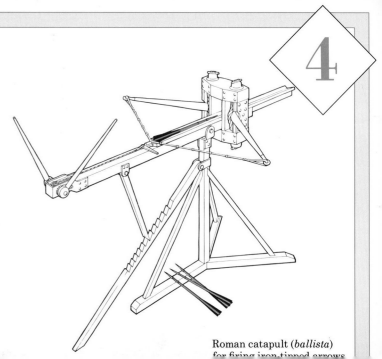

Roman catapult (*ballista*)
for firing iron-tipped arrows

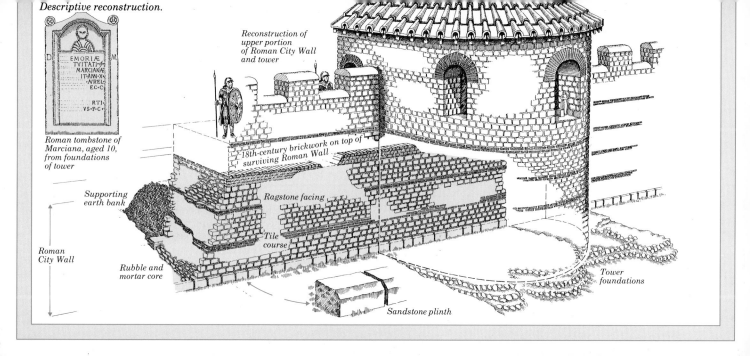

Descriptive reconstruction.

Roman tombstone of
Marciana, aged 10,
from foundations
of tower

Reconstruction of
upper portion
of Roman City Wall
and tower

18th-century brickwork on top of
surviving Roman Wall

Supporting
earth bank

Ragstone facing

Roman
City Wall

Tile
course

Rubble and
mortar core

Tower
foundations

Sandstone plinth

ALDGATE, *CITY GATE*

At road junction, on wall of Sir John Cass School

When the Roman City Wall was built (*c.*AD 200) a stone gate perhaps already spanned the Roman road linking London (*Londinium*) with Colchester (*Camulodunum*). The gate probably had twin entrances flanked by guard towers. Outside the gate a large cemetery developed to the south of the road. In the later 4th century the gate may have been rebuilt to provide a platform for catapults.

The Roman gate apparently survived until the medieval period (called *Alegate* or *Algate*) when it was rebuilt in 1108–47, and again in 1215. Its continued importance was assured by the building of the great Priory of Holy Trinity just inside the gate. The medieval gate had a single entrance flanked by two large semi-circular towers. It was during this period that Aldgate had its most famous resident, the poet Geoffrey Chaucer, who lived in rooms over the gate from 1374 while a customs official in the port of London.

Aldgate was completely rebuilt in 1607–9 but was finally pulled down in 1761 in order to improve traffic access.

Chaucer, from an edial reprint of the 'Canterbury Tales'

The Roman gateway at
Aldgate, seen from inside
the City *c.*AD 200.
Reconstruction.

CITY WALL

On subway wall

Excavations in 1977 for a subway under Duke's Place cut through the line of the City Wall, revealing Roman and medieval stonework. This section through the Wall has been marked by mosaic murals. The bottom ot the Wall which marks Roman ground level is now 14 feet (4.2m) below the modern street.

In the medieval period the area inside the City Wall was occupied by the important Augustinian Priory of Holy Trinity Aldgate, founded in 1108 by Queen Matilda, the wife of King Henry I. Archaeological excavations revealed a doorway which had been cut through the Wall. It was probably built to allow easy access to those properties owned by the Priory outside the Wall. As the level of the bottom of this doorway shows, the ground level had already risen by 7 feet (2.2m) by the medieval period. The doorway was blocked up in the 15th century.

The City Wall cut by a doorway of the Priory of Holy Trinity Aldgate, *below left*.

Section through the City Wall.

Battlements

Roman sentry walk

Modern street level

Subway ceiling

Medieval ground level

Earth bank

BEVIS MARKS, *CITY WALL*

On wall of 10–16 Bevis Marks

The engraving shows the area around Bevis Marks as it appeared (*c*.1560–70) in the reign of Elizabeth I. The City Wall, Aldgate, four towers and the City ditch can be clearly seen. Although the Wall has now disappeared in this area many of the streets still survive today.

Outside the Wall were wooden tenter frames used for stretching newly woven cloth (the origin of the phrase '*to be on tenter hooks*'). A gun foundry can also be seen near St Botolph's Church at the end of Houndsditch. Beyond were open fields (Spital Fields) stretching towards the villages of Shoreditch and Whitechapel.

The historian John Stow, writing *c*.1580 recorded the many unsuccessful attempts to prevent the City ditch becoming a dumping ground for rubbish including the dead dogs, which gave Houndsditch its name. In the 17th century the ditch was finally filled in and the area used for gardens.

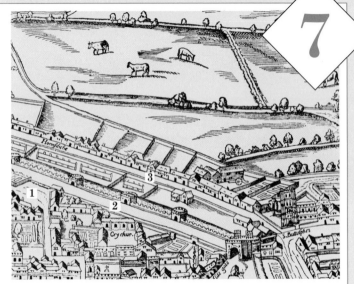

Bevis Marks and area: from the 'Agas' map *c*.1560–70.
1 Bevis Marks   2 City Wall   3 Houndsditch

BISHOPSGATE, *CITY GATE*

On north-east corner of Bishopsgate and Camomile Street

Bishopsgate Street preserves the line of one of the most important roads in Roman Britain, Ermine Street, which ran from London north to York (*Eburacum*) and then to Hadrian's Wall. The Roman gate has never been excavated but it probably had two entrance ways flanked by square guard towers.

The gate seems to have survived on the site until the Middle Ages and perhaps gained its name through an unknown association with the Bishop of London. The gate was rebuilt in 1479. The 16th-century engraving shows buildings stretching beyond the gate to the village of Shoreditch. Heads of criminals displayed on spikes above the gate gave a grisly warning.

In the medieval period all the gates were closed every evening after the curfew bell had been rung at the church of St Martin-le-Grand. In the daytime they provided a convenient point to check people entering the City and to take tolls to pay for the upkeep of the Wall or for other purposes. They also demonstrated the prestige of the City and it was for this reason that they survived after their defensive function had ceased.

The gateway at Bishopsgate in its final form: built 1735; demolished 1760. *18th-century engraving*.

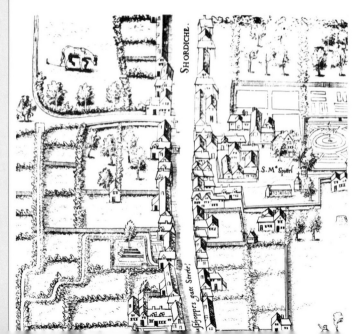

Bishopsgate: from the Copperplate Map c.1553–59.

Medieval Bishopsgate as rebuilt in 1479. *Reconstruction*.

Blak hows

Bedlame

Bedlam Gate

Giardin di Piero

S. Buriss

BVSSHOPPES GATE.

PAPYE

ST BOTOLPH, *CITY WALL*

In Bishopsgate Churchyard

The line of the City Wall is preserved by the back walls of the shops fronting on to Wormwood Street. Where the City Wall no longer acted as a defence it often survived as a property boundary. The shops here originated as a row of small buildings erected against the back of the City Wall in the late 17th century. The stone wall was gradually replaced by brickwork but the Wall as a property boundary prevented the buildings being extended northwards.

An 18th-century plan shows the ground floor of one of these shops built against the Wall. The inhabitants had already inserted a staircase and clearly there was every incentive to cut back into the City Wall to increase floorspace.

In the Middle Ages a church was founded outside Bishopsgate dedicated to St Botolph. Two other churches with the same dedication are positioned outside the gates at Aldgate and Aldersgate.

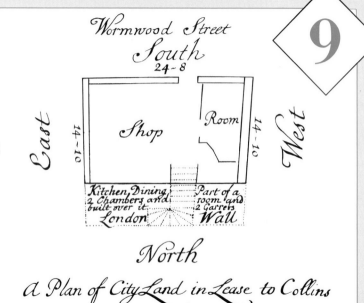

Plan of 18th-century building, used as a shop, built against the inside of the City Wall

The City Wall, *c.*1650, seen from outside with houses built against the inner face. *Reconstruction.*

ALL HALLOWS, *CITY WALL*

By entrance of All Hallows Church, London Wall

The present church was designed by George Dance the Younger in 1765. All Hallows was first built before 1100 as a small church against the surviving Roman City Wall. The churchyard wall of stone and brick is built on top of the City Wall. Excavations in 1905 revealed the Roman Wall with medieval stonework above, 13 feet (4m) below the present ground surface.

The excavations also showed that the shape of the vestry on the northern side of the church was determined by the semi-circular foundations of a Roman tower. This tower was one of a series added to the Wall on the eastern side of the City in the late Roman period. In the Middle Ages it was used as a dwelling for a religious hermit (anchorite) for whom All Hallows was famous. These recluses were walled-up in small cells and survived only on food and alms given by passers-by.

O̶r̶de my god I desyre to laude the / for I knowe mysffe to be made to laude þ. Open my mouth in thy laude þ I may synge Joye to thy name. Stere my hert in the / put away euery tedyous thynge / infunde grace / kendle

Simon the Anker, hermit at All Hallows, praying to a patron saint. *Woodcut of 1514*

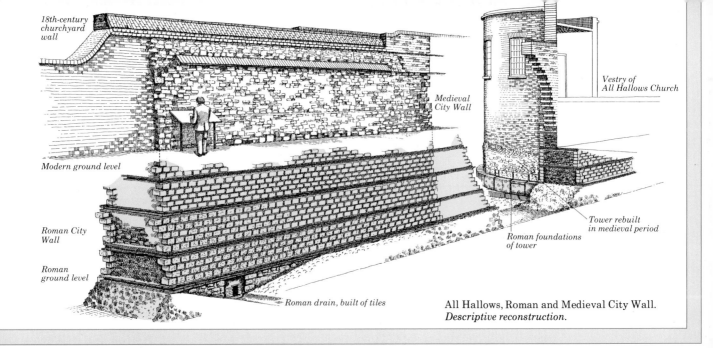

18th-century
churchyard
wall

Medieval
City Wall

Vestry of
All Hallows Church

Modern ground level

Roman City
Wall

Roman
ground level

Tower rebuilt
in medieval period

Roman foundations
of tower

Roman drain, built of tiles

All Hallows, Roman and Medieval City Wall.
Descriptive reconstruction.

MOORGATE, *CITY GATE*

At north-east corner of junction of Moorgate and London Wall

Moorgate was the only gate whose name described its location as it gave access to the moor or marsh which stretched along the northern side of the City. In the early Roman period the area was well-drained by the Walbrook stream but the construction of the City Wall (*c*.AD 200) impeded the natural drainage and caused the formation of a large marsh outside the Wall.

There was no Roman gate here but in the Middle Ages a small gate was built. In 1415 it was totally rebuilt by the Mayor Thomas Falconer and the engraving shows it after substantial rebuilding as a single gate, flanked by towers. Throughout the 16th century attempts were made to drain the marsh and within a hundred years the whole area had been laid out with walks and avenues of trees. In 1672 Moorgate was rebuilt as an imposing ceremonial entrance. This was demolished to improve traffic access in 1761. The City Wall to the east became incorporated into the Bethlehem Hospital (*Bedlam*) for the insane. This long stretch of the Wall was finally demolished in 1817.

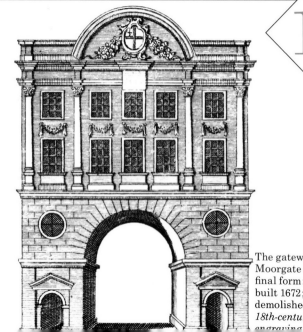

The gateway at Moorgate in its final form: built 1672; demolished 1761. *18th-century engraving*

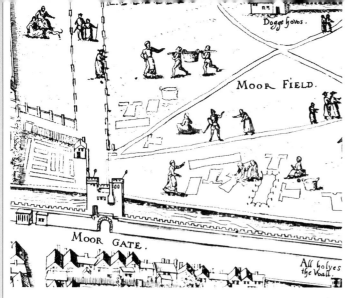

Moorgate: from the Copperplate Map
c.1553–59.

The medieval City Wall, surviving as the boundary wall (right) of
the Bethlehem Hospital. *Engraving of 1814.*

ST ALPHEGE, *CITY WALL*

In the gardens at St Alphege

This section originally formed the northern wall of the Roman fort built *c*.AD 120 and it subsequently became incorporated into the line of the Roman City Wall. The Wall decayed during the Saxon period and in the 11th century a church dedicated to St Alphege was built with the City Wall as its northern side. The church was demolished in the 16th century.

The Wall shows a number of rebuildings and repairs. On the northern (outer) side are two distinct types of stone facing. The later work, to the west, uses knapped flints and pieces of tile as decorative bands in the stonework. During the Wars of the Roses the Mayor Ralph Joceline ordered large-scale repairs to the Wall between Aldgate and Aldersgate in 1477, and it was probably at this time that the battlements at St Alphege were rebuilt in red bricks.

The Wall later became incorporated into buildings, and cellars were cut into it leaving a core only 18 inches (0.45m) thick at the western end.

Roman, Medieval and later City Wall in St Alphege churchyard
exposed after World War II damage

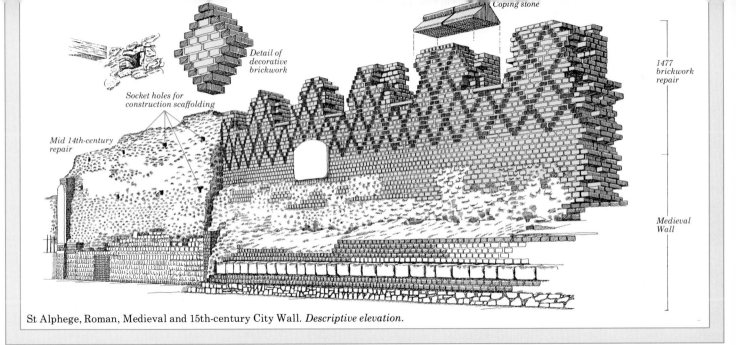

Coping stone

Detail of decorative brickwork

Socket holes for construction scaffolding

Mid 14th-century repair

1477 brickwork repair

Medieval Wall

St Alphege, Roman, Medieval and 15th-century City Wall. *Descriptive elevation.*

CRIPPLEGATE, *CITY GATE*

13

On corner of Wood Street and St Alphege Garden

Cripplegate was originally the northern entrance to the
Roman fort, built *c*.AD 120. This Roman gate probably
remained in use until at least the late Saxon period when it
is mentioned in 10th and 11th century documents. The gate
was rebuilt in the 1490s. Throughout its history Cripplegate
had a variety of uses. It was leased as accommodation and
also, like the more famous Newgate, used as a prison.

After the restoration of Charles II in 1660 all of the City
gates were unhinged and the portcullises wedged open
making them useless for defence. The gates survived another
century as ceremonial entrances before being demolished.

Cripplegate gave access to a substantial medieval suburb
and to the village of Islington. Extra defensive works
outside the gate gave rise to the name Barbican which was
subsequently taken as the name for the post World War II
rebuilding of the area.

Medieval Cripplegate, as it appeared after rebuilding in 1491,

Cripplegate, seen from inside
the City in the late Saxon period,
c.AD 900. *Reconstruction*.

CITY WALL AND TOWERS

In churchyard, to south of St Giles Cripplegate

This section of the Wall originally formed the northern side of the Roman fort, built *c*.AD 120. The defences were completely rebuilt in the early medieval period and most of the surviving stonework dates to this time.

The modern lake indicates the approximate position of the medieval ditch, which then contained a '*great store of verie good fish, of diverse sorts.*' In the 13th century a series of towers was added to the outside of the Wall and the remains of two such towers survive here. The battlements in this section were rebuilt in brick probably in the late 15th century as at St Alphege.

From the early medieval period there grew up a suburb outside the Wall around the church of St Giles founded *c*.1090. After the ditch was filled in during the 17th century the City Wall became the southern boundary of the churchyard. This ensured the survival of the Wall until 1803 when, '*by reason of the frequent nuisances committed by some of the louest class of people, who had been suffered to inhabit the adjoining premises*', it was demolished.

The battlements of the City Wall in the churchyard of St Giles, as they appeared in 1793 shortly before demolition. *Engraving of 1812.*

St Giles Cripplegate, Medieval City Wall and towers.
Descriptive reconstruction.

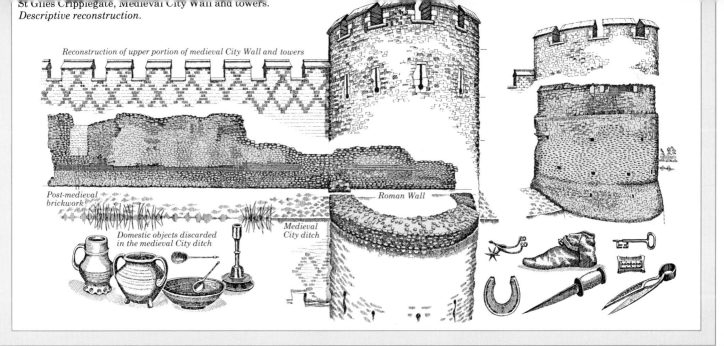

Reconstruction of upper portion of medieval City Wall and towers

Post-medieval brickwork

Roman Wall

Domestic objects discarded in the medieval City ditch

Medieval City ditch

ST GILES CRIPPLEGATE, *TOWER*

At north end of gardens by east side of Museum of London

This medieval tower marks the north-west corner of the Roman and medieval defences. Most of the Roman Wall was completely rebuilt in the early medieval period. In 1211–13 a new defensive ditch was dug around the outside of the Wall and soon after a series of towers was added along its western side. This tower survives to two-thirds of its original height. It would have had wooden floors.

In peacetime the towers were rented for a variety of uses and some were occupied by hermits. This tower may have been used for this purpose since in the 13th century the hermitage of St James in the Wall was built nearby. In 1872, when the area was redeveloped, the crypt of the hermitage chapel was removed to Mark Lane where it still survives.

Although the City ditch was eventually filled in and the churchyard of St Giles was extended up to the Wall, the tower survived. It became almost buried in earth dumped to raise the level of the churchyard, but was uncovered during the Barbican redevelopment of the 1960s.

The medieval tower at St Giles Cripplegate in a modern setting, *below*

The medieval tower in the churchyard
of St Giles, *above.*
Redrawn from a 19th-century engraving.

The medieval tower as exposed by bomb
damage in World War II.

BARBER-SURGEONS' HALL, *TOWER*

In gardens to east side of Museum, by Barber-Surgeons' Hall

Along this stretch of the defences much of the Roman Wall was rebuilt in the early medieval period. Towers were added in the 13th century. This tower, of which only the lower levels survive, was originally similar in appearance to those towers on either side.

During the medieval period, the area inside the Wall was used as gardens but by the 16th century buildings started to encroach on the Wall. In 1607 the Barber-Surgeons' Company, whose livery hall was near the tower, built a courtroom which incorporated the tower as an apse at its western end.

North of the courtroom more buildings were added in the 1630s, including an anatomy theatre, designed by Inigo Jones. The hall was badly damaged in the Great Fire of 1666, but was rebuilt. These buildings were in turn partly demolished in 1863–4 and were completely destroyed by bombing in 1940. The Wall, to the north of the tower, with its stone and brickwork patching dating from the 12th to 19th centuries, reflects these many alterations. In 1969 the present Barber-Surgeons' Hall was opened by her Majesty Queen Elizabeth the Queen Mother.

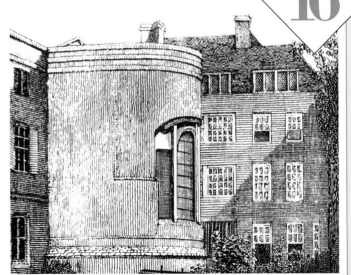

The medieval tower incorporated into the Barber-Surgeons' Hall, as viewed from St Giles' churchyard. *Engraving of 1800.*

The buildings of the Barber-Surgeons'
Company and surrounding area seen
from outside the Wall *c.*1750.
Reconstruction.

CITY WALL & MEDIEVAL TOWER

On west side of Wall, in gardens on east side of Museum

This section formed the west side of the Roman fort, built *c.*AD 120, later strengthened and incorporated into the Roman city defences, *c.*AD 200. In the early medieval period the Roman Wall was extensively rebuilt and in 1257 Henry III '*caused the walles of this Cities, which was sore decaied and destitute of towers, to be repaired in more seemely wise than before.*' At this time several towers were added to the Wall on the City's western side.

This tower was probably originally three storeys high and the remains of several arrow slits can be seen. During the later medieval period several of the towers and gates were let as houses and this tower was converted into a simple dwelling.

During the 18th century houses were built against the outside of the Wall and the tower disappeared from view. As the whole area changed from residential to industrial use in the 19th century sections of the medieval stone wall were demolished and replaced by brick. The destruction of the surrounding buildings by bombing in 1940 revealed the tower again.

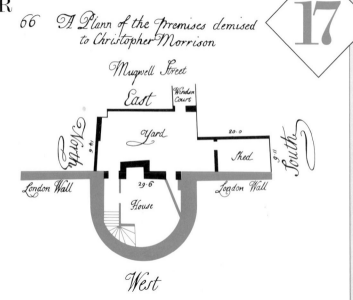

66 *A Plann of the Premises demised to Christopher Morrison*

Plan of the medieval tower converted into a small 18th-century house

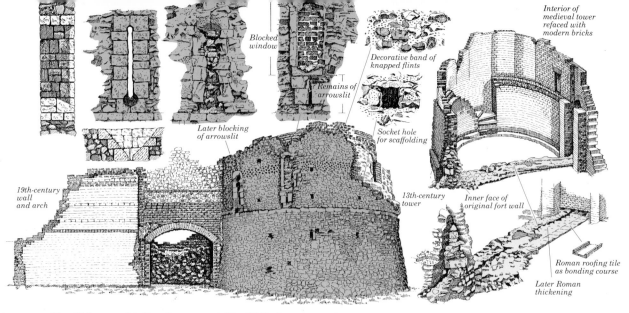

Blocked window

Remains of arrowslit

Later blocking of arrowslit

Decorative band of knapped flints

Socket hole for scaffolding

Interior of medieval tower refaced with modern bricks

19th-century wall and arch

13th-century tower

Inner face of original fort wall

Roman roofing tile as bonding course

Later Roman thickening

Garden on east side of Museum, Medieval tower and City Wall. *Descriptive elevation.*

WEST GATE OF ROMAN FORT

Below London Wall at Bastion House. Opening times restricted

Prior to the construction of the western section of the road London Wall in 1959, excavations revealed the west gate of the Roman fort, built *c*.AD 120. It had twin entrance ways flanked on either side by square towers.

Only the northern tower can now be seen. It provided a guardroom and access to the sentry walk along the Wall. Large blocks of sandstone formed the base, some weighing over half a ton (500kg). The remaining masonry consisted of ragstone brought from Kent. The guardroom opened on to a gravel road, which was divided into two by stone piers supporting the arches spanning the gates. Each passage was wide enough for a cart and had a pair of heavy wooden doors.

Running northwards from the gate-tower is the fort wall, 4 feet (1.2m) thick with the internal thickening added when the fort was incorporated into the Roman city defences *c*.AD 200. The gate was eventually blocked, probably in the troubled years of the later 4th century. By the medieval period the site of the gate had been completely forgotten.

Roman gate at Newgate, similar in style to the Fort Gate.
Reconstruction below.

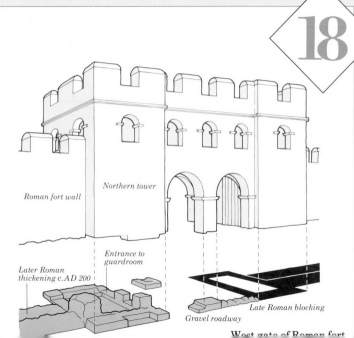

Roman fort wall

Northern tower

Later Roman thickening c.AD 200

Entrance to guardroom

Gravel roadway

Late Roman blocking

West gate of Roman fort

ROMAN FORT AND CITY WALL

At north end of Noble Street

This section shows the base of the Roman City Wall. It supports a 19th-century brick boundary wall which still preserves its line. The Roman foundations consist of two parallel walls, the inner one being slightly thicker and later in date. The outer wall is the foundation of the west wall of the Roman fort, built c.AD 120. It perhaps originally stood to a height of over 15 feet (4.5m). Access to the sentry walk was by several small square turrets on the inner face of the Wall. The foundations of one of these is visible here.

When the fort was incorporated into the City defences c.AD 200, a thickening was added to strengthen the Wall and it was probably heightened at the same time. Part of the core of this thickening still survives to a height of 8 feet (2.4m) with ragstone laid in herringbone courses. Above this can be seen the medieval rebuilding. The outer face of the Wall shows different medieval building techniques, one to the south using courses of stone alternating with layers of tiles.

The City Wall and internal turret of the Roman fort, during excavations, *below*.

Roman fort wall

Later Roman thickening

Medieval facings: tile and stonework

Medieval rebuilding

Foundation of internal turret

19th-century brick wall

Base of Roman fort wall

Noble Street, Roman fort and City Wall. *Descriptive elevation*

ROMAN FORT AND CITY WALL

At south end of Noble Street

A fort occupying an area of about 12 acres was built on the north-west edge of the Roman city c.AD 120. It had a gate in each side and would probably have conformed to the common Roman rectangular fort plan.

The fort was probably built to house the official guard of the Governor of Britain, who was based in London. At least 1,000 men, cavalry and infantry, would have been housed in the fort's barrack blocks around the central range of administrative buildings and stores.

The walls surviving here form the curved south-west corner of the fort with the foundations of a rectangular corner watch-tower. The fort wall was originally about 4 feet (1.2m) thick and at least 15 feet (4.5m) high.

When the Roman City Wall was built c.AD 200, two sides of the fort were incorporated into the City's defences. The City Wall (left), 9 feet (2.7m) thick, joins the south-west corner of the fort. Along the western and northern sides of the fort an extra thickening was added to the inside of the wall to bring it up to the standard strength.

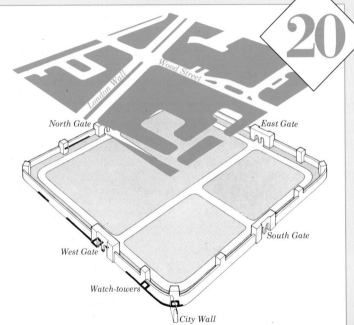

The area of the Roman fort and its relationship to modern streets.

The Roman fort and City Wall,
seen from the southwest
c.AD 200. *Reconstruction.*

ALDERSGATE, *CITY GATE*

On railings on east side of Aldersgate

The increasing threat of raids by Saxons from across the North Sea in the 4th century led to the strengthening of the City defences. It was probable that the west gate of the Roman fort was blocked and a new gate was built here at this time. This gate was of late Roman military design with twin roadways flanked by semi-circular projecting towers. These were built of solid masonry and provided an elevated platform for catapults.

Aldersgate continued as an important gate in the medieval period as it gave access beyond the Wall and ditch to St Bartholomew's Priory, the London Charterhouse and the livestock market and fair on Smithfield. It was also sometimes used as a prison. On 20 October 1660 Samuel Pepys wrote '*I saw the limbs of some of our new trytors, set upon Aldersgate . . . A bloody week this and the last have been, there being ten hanged, drawn and quartered.*'

After being damaged in the Great Fire of 1666 the gate was rebuilt. This imposing structure was finally demolished in 1761 to improve traffic access.

21

The gateway at Aldersgate in its final form: built 1672; demolished 1760. *18th-century*

The late Roman gateway at
Aldersgate, seen from outside
the City *c*.AD 375.
Reconstruction.

ACKNOWLEDGEMENTS

Original Panel design: The Partners

Reconstruction drawings on
Panels 1, 5, 8, 9, 13, 16, 20 and 21:
Peter Jackson

Elevation drawings on
Panels 2, 3, 4, 10, 12, 14, 17 and 19:
Graham Evernden

Other drawings:
David Penny, Richard Sorrell

Photographs:
Barrington Gray, John Edwards,
Trevor Hurst, Jon Bailey

General map:
Reproduced by kind permission of
Ordnance Survey,
Crown copyright reserved.

The London Wall Walk was made possible
by the following sponsors:

City Parochial Foundation
Coopers & Lybrand
Cornhill Insurance PLC
Cripplegate Foundation
Robert Dyas Ltd
European Ferries PLC
Land Securities PLC
Lloyd's Register of Shipping
Midland Bank PLC
Norton, Rose, Botterell & Roche
Phillips & Drew
The Esmée Fairbairn Charitable Trust
The Post Office
Tower Hill Improvement Trust
Worshipful Company of Barbers

Designed by Cedric Knight
Printed and bound in England by
Balding + Mansell Limited

ISBN 0 904818 13 6